MW01068673

G.R.A.C.E. at Work Handbook

Quick Guide to Great Relationships

2nd Edition

Eric de Nijs

GRACE Press

ISBN: 978-0-9833403-2-4 (ebook version)
      978-0-9833403-3-1 *(print version)*

Second Edition

Published by:

GRACE Press
Henrico, Virginia

http://www.graceatwork.com

Dedication

*As always, this book is dedicated to my wife,
Nancy, who is the sunshine of my life.*

*I may have developed G.R.A.C.E. at Work,
but it is Nancy who taught me how it really works and
enabled our relationship to be G.R.A.C.E.-full.*

Words cannot express my thanks, and my love.

Foreword

The military started offering senior officers the opportunity to enlist the service of an "Executive Coach" a few years back to deal with the unconventional, and at times severe stress we deal with in America's All Volunteer Force. I needed the help attacking the task I had of re-establishing the U.S. Navy's Second Fleet and establishing NATO's Joint Force Command Norfolk. I was truly blessed to enjoy the services of Dr. Eric de Nijs as my executive coach.

Being a commander in the military is like being the CEO of a company in our free market, but there are differences. First, commanders are assigned for 2-3 years at a time and each command is different. In my case, I had command six times from commander of a single F/A-18 squadron to an entire fleet and NATO command simultaneously. Military officers get one chance at command at each level. Second, the commander is responsible for everything that goes on whether he or she can directly influence the circumstances.

All military officers who are honored with the opportunity to command, in peace or war, are students of leadership. The cost of failure is too high. Addition to reading books on leadership, studying the performance of others, an executive coach is another resource of a leader.

Eric is neither a former military officer nor versed in military culture. That is precisely why he is so effective as a coach and confidante'. The principles found in the G.R.A.C.E. Handbook are applicable to any organization at any time. They are derived from the Truth found in the Bible. Goodwill, Results, Authenticity, Connectivity, and Empowerment are attributes found in perfection in only one person who ever walked this earth, Jesus Christ Himself. The handbook applies these concepts in a practical and objective way, and it starts with Relationships that lead to Connectivity.

Eric and I had numerous weighty discussions over the two plus years we worked together, and he is a remarkable listener and confidante'. Most conversations would not be appropriate to recount. However, one conversation is illustrative of his clarity of thought. When the commands were quickly expanding in number of personnel from the original twelve individuals to over 200 in each command, Eric gently coaxed me into recruiting people very deliberately. He said, "There are three types of people you need in the command: "Proactive, Co-Active, and Active."

When you had twelve people, you needed a large percentage of Proactive (close advisors and disruptive thinkers) people. Now, most of your people should be Active (Sailors that do the real work) while there are fewer Co-Active (NCOs and mid-grade officers) and Proactive people. I won't forget that conversation!

This short handbook is worth reading and referencing when leading any organization.

Andrew L. Lewis

Vice Admiral, USN (retired)

Table of Contents

Everything begins with
Goodwill. There are
consequences, either
intended or not, that will
result from every word we
speak, and every action we
take. This is why it is so
important to start and end
every conversation, every
action, with Goodwill.

When Goodwill is present
in all words and deeds,
the message sent is that
someone took the time to
care, listen, and explore
with Goodwill. Sometimes
this is all it takes to
open the floodgates of
opportunity.

The G.R.A.C.E. at Work Handbook

Relationships = Connections

Anytime we connect
with anyone else, for any reason,
we enter into a relationship of some sort.

The size and success of those relationships
(whether with one other, or several others) will
depend on how we communicate with each other.
Communication can come in many ways - through
conversation, through our actions, and through our
attitudes. Great relationships are based on great
communication. This is true whether in business,
professional, or personal relationships. There are
certain ways that people act with one another
(communication) that are known to work well. And,
there are others known not to work so well!

G.R.A.C.E. at Work is a relationship model that
was created after years of watching the kind of
communication that brings successful results to
relationships. It's basically about how people work
best together. We call this "human dynamics." The
same principles will work with all humans...*well,
most of them!*

One of the basic ideas of G.R.A.C.E. at Work
is that everything in life happens through
conversation and relationships. Every conversation
is an opportunity to build a relationship or tear it

down. That involves a choice on our part. When we choose to use the G.R.A.C.E. at Work model in our relationships, we are growing the potential of the relationship. We call this "Playing in a Bigger Space." Although this is a little book, it is filled with some very powerful ways to have great relationships that allow you to achieve great results, and play in a much bigger space.

The Power of G.R.A.C.E.

The idea behind the word "grace" works well with this model. Grace generally brings to mind two ideas. One is undeserved favor. In other words, we are treated much better than we deserve. The other is an elegance in movement. Both of these ideas contribute to communicating with grace.

G.R.A.C.E. at Work *assumes Goodwill*, which will sometimes require undeserved favor. And this kind of relationship is not always pain free or even easy. It takes effort, commitment and yes, grace. But the anticipation and realization of success is well worth any short-term pain and difficulty.

It's Not About Me

There is a basic concept about the G.R.A.C.E. at Work model that must be understood. It is not about you, or me, *it is about all of us*. This is not always popular among many people today, but it is absolutely necessary for G.R.A.C.E-full relationships.

The success of relationships sometimes requires individual sacrifice. And that may mean doing what's best for others, instead of pushing the best for self. In the game of baseball, a sacrifice fly or bunt may result in a player sacrificing his personal performance statistics to advance the team. Similarly, a sacrifice in a relationship may mean that a person gives up his or her agenda, his or her need to be "right," or the need to be first. This is the pure meaning of Goodwill.

Must Have #1: It Always Begins with Goodwill

The basis for the model G.R.A.C.E. at Work, from the start to the finish, is Goodwill. Goodwill can be defined as a kindly feeling of approval and support, interest or concern, cheerful consent, and willing effort. Any of these definitions requires effort and a deliberate commitment to work within the relationship with Goodwill toward all concerned. For this reason, Goodwill is the first and foremost part in the G.R.A.C.E at Home model. Without it, relationships fail, and communication hits a brick wall.

Must Have #2: Trust

A foundation of trust is one of the most important things that shows the strength of a relationship. Trust means placing confidence or belief in someone or something. This creates an environment where there is trust for all people in the relationship.

Trust always thinks good rather than bad of people, and of situations. It is about giving trust, and encouraging trust. Trust is being confident about the character, ability, strength, or truth of someone or something. Trust must have a healthy back-and-forth place to thrive. Great relationships start with trust, and build on trust.

Must Have #3: Shared Purpose
People are in relationships for a reason. They expect to get certain results, which is the purpose of the relationship. But if those reasons are not shared, we are not working together, and will most likely not achieve the results we want. This means everyone in the relationship must know the desired results, and share equally in the purpose of being together in relationship.

Relationships are always dynamic, or they are not really a relationship. They are either growing or dying; there is no such thing as a static *(not moving)* relationship. As the relationship grows, shared purpose may change, but it allows a relationship to move and grow, and is the reason behind the need for good communication.

The "Click" Factor
We've all had those relationships where we "clicked" with people - when everything about the relationship just felt right. It's that special

connection with certain people that lets us be who we really are. We share a common purpose, we tend to trust more and are more likely to forgive and forget when needed. We also will more rapidly give and receive. We are most likely practicing G.R.A.C.E. at Work.

Can you remember a powerful relationship in your life where you just seemed to "click" with the other person **click!** or group? You can't really put your finger on it, but for some reason you just felt right, comfortable and accepted. You simply "clicked."

Think of one of your relationships where you could say "we just clicked." How would you describe this relationship? Chances are very good that you would include the parts and pieces of the G.R.A.C.E. at Work model. "Click" is not coincidental or accidental. It happens when we practice G.R.A.C.E., which makes relationships powerful, productive, and satisfying.

The Safe Place of G.R.A.C.E.

G.R.A.C.E. at Work makes a safe place for people to be and act - within boundaries - without fear of failure. It is a place for people to share their deepest feelings, their weaknesses, and their hopes and desires. It also gives them the chance to learn new things in a safe place.

Without G.R.A.C.E., relationships are only a series of "transactions" *(taking care of "business")*. These don't satisfy anyone and won't usually give you the results you want. The safe space of G.R.A.C.E. turns transactions into *transformations*, where real change happens and everyone grows.

A relationship, whether business, professional or personal, will either be transactional, or transformational.

Transaction or Transformation?

So what's the difference between these two? Plenty. One defines a flat stagnant relationship and the other one is filled with shared success.

Transaction: an act, process or activity where two or more people handle something that concerns both of them.

Transformation: a change, usually for the better, in anything or anyone. Used here it is more about inward change of heart, thought, and condition.

Transformational Relationship

Transactional Relationship

When something is transactional, it only involves the basic needs of any necessary activity. When something is transformational, it changes something or someone.

The transactional relationship does not have any of what we call a *"click"* factor or what seems to make relationships work (they just "click"). It is all about compliance (following the rules, doing the basic needs). The transformational relationship has commitment of the partners to get results. It changes people by letting them dream, explore, face problems, heal, grow and celebrate together through the five parts of G.R.A.C.E. at Work.

In order for G.R.A.C.E. at Work to really work well, it needs people to have a sense of "open doors" and opportunities to make a choice to show Goodwill. The G.R.A.C.E. at Work model gives the framework for relationships that are committed, not just compliant. But all these plans on paper mean nothing until people breathe life into them. Don't just know or talk about G.R.A.C.E. at Work. Use it to give your relationships life and to realize bigger and more powerful results.

The Safe Place of G.R.A.C.E.

TRANSACTIONAL Relationship	**TRANSFORMATIONAL** Relationship
COMPLIANCE	**COMMITMENT**
"CLICK" Missing	**"CLICK"** Present

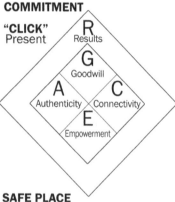

NO SAFE PLACE Absence of G.R.A.C.E.	**SAFE PLACE** **Presence of G.R.A.C.E.**
GROWTH POTENTIAL: NONE - DEAD END	**GROWTH POTENTIAL:** **UNLIMITED OPPORTUNITY**

G.R.A.C.E. at Work: The BASICS

G.R.A.C.E. at Work is a very simple *(but powerful)*, interactive model that helps build trust and openness needed for successful relationships.

Strong and powerful relationships only happen when all the parts of G.R.A.C.E. at Work are present and practiced by everyone.

The G.R.A.C.E. at Work model is shown as a diamond "on point," with four diamonds inside. There is always a reason for relationships, and people are expecting certain results (The "R" part of G.R.A.C.E.). For this reason the other four diamonds are contained inside the bigger "R" (Results) diamond. Inside each of the 5 parts of G.R.A.C.E. are 7 smaller "pieces." For example, Goodwill, the first part, has seven pieces to it that are required to make the entire Goodwill part work. *(See diagram page 17.)*

The Parts of G.R.A.C.E.

The results you get from any relationship will depend on the amount and balance of all the parts of G.R.A.C.E. at Work. If one part, or even one piece to any part is missing *(or not in balance with others)*, desired results will fall short of your expectations.

G.R.A.C.E. at Work (G.A.W.) was developed over the years by carefully watching how human relationships work together to get the best results. We call this process "human dynamics." When the parts of G.R.A.C.E., especially Goodwill, are present in any relationship from the start, relationships grow and produce results even beyond those hoped for.

The complete G.A.W. model is shown on the next page, with all five parts and the seven pieces of each part. Note the numbers, such as "G1" for "Positivism" under Goodwill, "A3" for "Responsibility/ Accountability" under Authenticity, and so on. The seven pieces of each of the five parts are referenced in this way (G1, G2 etc.).

Brief descriptions of all the pieces of the 5 parts follow on the next pages.

The <u>Pieces</u> of G.R.A.C.E.

GOODWILL
G1: Positivism
G2: Non-Judgment
G3: Support
G4: Giving Freely
G5: Forgiveness
G6: Peace
G7: Gratitude

RESULTS
R1: Shared Purpose
R2: Desired Outcomes
R3: Why/Who Balance
R4: Known Assumptions
R5: Mutual Contribution
R6: Action Plans
R7: Performance

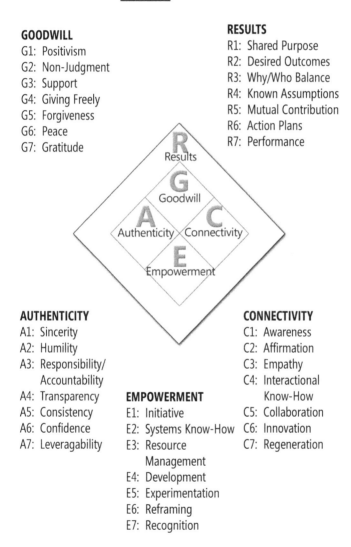

AUTHENTICITY
A1: Sincerity
A2: Humility
A3: Responsibility/
     Accountability
A4: Transparency
A5: Consistency
A6: Confidence
A7: Leveragability

EMPOWERMENT
E1: Initiative
E2: Systems Know-How
E3: Resource
     Management
E4: Development
E5: Experimentation
E6: Reframing
E7: Recognition

CONNECTIVITY
C1: Awareness
C2: Affirmation
C3: Empathy
C4: Interactional
     Know-How
C5: Collaboration
C6: Innovation
C7: Regeneration

GOODWILL: It All Begins Here

The foundation for G.R.A.C.E., from the start and all the way to the finish, is Goodwill. Goodwill sets the stage for a trusting relationship. When Goodwill is not present from the start, trust won't be either. And without Goodwill and trust, you won't be able to reach the goals you desire for the relationship.

The PIECES of Goodwill...

G1: Positivism

Being and thinking in a positive (not negative) way. Being positive or negative about things is a choice. In this first piece of Goodwill, we choose to start with positive *intent* about everything, everyone, and every situation. Every relationship which begins and continues in this way has a much better chance of succeeding and reaching desired goals. Along the way there will be bumps. Will you approach these bumps by being positive, or negative?

G2: Non-Judgment

This is about not judging people or situations. It is our natural way to judge, so this one is hard sometimes. We make a choice to hold off on judgment and not allow our own values, expectations, ideas or personal bias to get in the way. Instead of judging, we try to find answers, not blame. We all have our way of thinking about things, and it is important to push that aside and remain open, positive and ready to understand. Pointing fingers never works in relationships; finding ways to make things work, does.

G3: Support

Having an attitude of kindness toward others, so that you are always there to support them and look out for their best interests. It is about being ready and willing to support others, in every way you can. It's not just something you do, but something you feel. You know their needs and desires, and do whatever you can to help them meet their goals. You honestly want them to grow and succeed. It's about helping others be all they can be.

G4: Giving Freely

Giving freely without expecting something in return. You are open-handed (not tight fisted), meaning what you have you want to give to others, whether it is things, or yourself. You want to share freely what you have to give. It might be sharing your time, what you know, your words or physical things. It is a desire to make others happy by giving whatever you have to give – no hidden agendas, no strings attached.

G5: Forgiveness

Giving up the need for revenge, repayment of any loss, or hard feelings. You are able to forgive something wrong done to you, without needing something back from the person. This is not just words, but a heart that doesn't hold a grudge and can go on without hard feelings. Like all the other pieces of this part, forgiveness is a choice we make to let go of hurts and move forward in Goodwill.

G6: Peace

Having a sense of calm and quiet inside. Not always fighting things you can't change. Wanting everyone to get along and have that same sense of peace. That means we are OK with the way things are, not wanting to always change someone or something. It means having a peace about self, others and situations. It's also about working through struggles and disagreements so everyone can be at peace again.

G7: Gratitude

Looking for ways to be thankful in all situations. Understanding that even in times of trouble, there is much to be thankful for. Also being able to express your thanks to others. We can be thankful for people, for relationships, for opportunities, and even for troubles that can help us grow and mature.

RESULTS: Why We're In This

A relationship will not have good results if everyone in the relationship does not know exactly what they want to get out of it, or the real reasons for the relationship. Only one piece of this part is about the planning it takes to get your wanted results. It is more about making sure everyone knows what they want, knows what the others want, and share their thoughts about these things. A good relationship does not just want results for self, but also truly desires results for everyone in the relationship.

The PIECES of Results...

R:1 Shared Purpose

People in a relationship believe in what they are doing together. But without sharing with one another what they want from the relationship, they will not know what the other person is thinking, and results will be different than what is desired. All people in the relationship need to know and understand why they are doing what they are doing, and agree together on the purpose of the relationship. And this is not just about what they want, but *why* they want it. In this piece everything about what and why is shared, so there can be no "hidden agendas" or "ulterior motives." It is coming together and joining (connecting) in understanding in order to get results each person desires.

R:2 Desired Outcomes

After each person shares their purpose for being in the relationship, and agreement is reached, each person needs to share what those results will look like. We can say why we are in the relationship, or what we hope to get out of it, but sometimes those things look different to different people. We need to be specific about the desired results. What, exactly, do they look like? How can they be measured or seen by others? Everyone should understand what these are, agree on them, and be able to work together to get these specific results for each person.

R3: Why/Who Balance

Relationships have two parts. One is the "why" which is the reason and hoped for results of the relationship. This could be a project, a marriage, or just because two people want to enjoy the other's company. The other part of relationships is the "who" - the people who have come together to fulfill the "why" of it. Both parts have value, to fulfill the reason, and to build up the people at the same time. This means that throughout the relationship everyone is looking for ways to build up the others in relationship, while accomplishing the purpose of the relationship. How can we bring value to others in relationship, even beyond the shared purpose and desired outcomes? It is a sincere desire to help make the lives of others in the relationship better, in small ways and in big ways. At the same time, the "why" of the relationship needs to have equal priority. We work together to accomplish the *purpose* of the relationship while building up the *people* of the relationship.

WHY (Reason for relationship)	WHO (People in relationship)
• What we're together for	• Needs of people
• What we need to do	• Building up, making better

R4: Known Assumptions

Assumptions are things that we think are true *(and take "for granted")*. They are the things we accept as truth, sometimes without proof. Because of the unknowns (about others) in new relationships, assumptions must be shared, talked out and then matched up with the beliefs of others. We need to make sure we have all our facts straight. Sometimes these need to be changed a little. It's important to know that assumptions (things we believe are true) aren't always true. *(Note: This is NOT about faith, but about the things people believe about a relationship or a person.)* Sometimes we believe things for a variety of reasons even though they may not be true. Things we believe to be true can also change from time to time and may need to be talked about again. To give any relationship the best possible chance to arrive at desired results, these need to be shared openly. This will avoid a lot of misunderstandings and troubles down the road.

R5: Mutual/Equal Contribution

People in relationship need to know that everyone will give, contribute and deliver on their commitments. This means everyone is doing their part, to get the results wanted. Mutual (or equal) contribution is a term to describe the agreement and understanding that everyone in the relationship will do his or her part, to the best of his or her ability. This means no slacking and letting others do all the work. It is working together in equal parts.

R6: Action Plans

To get the results we want, we need to have some sort of plan. *How will we work together? What exactly will we do to work toward our desired results?* An action plan simply means how will we act and what will we do to get our results. It needs to talk about who does what, by when, and how. This plan includes responsibilities, and being answerable about them. This means everyone understands what they are to do, and others are expecting them to do these things. They will also be willing to explain, and if necessary, defend, their actions. Action plans are not secret. Everyone needs to know the plan, so everyone can contribute what they are responsible for. It is sometimes best to write down an action plan so everyone is on the same page.

R7: Performance

You've already shared your purpose, talked about your desired outcomes, decided you would like to improve the value of the relationship for others, talked about what you all know and believe about things, agreed to work together in equal amounts, and come up with a plan to get your results. This is now the "work" of the relationship to get the outcomes you want. And while you are doing the work, you will want to check in frequently to make sure you are still on the right track. It's about measuring how well the work is going, and deciding if you need to make any changes to make it work better.

AUTHENTICITY: Being Real

Authenticity is being real *(not phony)*. You are who you are, you say exactly what you mean, and use the same standards with others *(the way you judge others)* as you do with yourself. Authenticity is not just about "walking the talk," it's about talking the *truth* and walking the *truth*—about yourself.

Real authenticity means being and doing *(thinking, speaking and acting)* in the same way all the time, a way that is true to who we really are. Authenticity is the very center and heart of the G.R.A.C.E. at Work model. All the other parts get their strength from this place of honesty.

The PIECES of Authenticity...

A1: Sincerity
Being real and speaking truthfully about personal feelings, thoughts and desires – showing others the real you. No deception, no lies, not being two-faced. It is the wish to communicate with earnestness and honesty. It is honesty in speaking and doing.

A2: Humility
Being modest about self, not prideful or arrogant, not thinking you are better or more important than anyone else. Being "down to earth," (not pretending). You can't fake this. Others will always know if you are really humble or just putting on an act. Humility can be seen in your attitude, words and actions.

A3: Responsibility/Accountability

Able to accept responsibility and then to back up your actions. It means you will do what you say you will do, and explain your actions and choices. Being able and willing to give honest reasons for personal behavior. No excuses, no blaming and no phony explanations. This means you are reliable and trustworthy.

A4: Transparency

A "transparent" person can be "seen through," with nothing hidden or in the way, and no "fakery." This person is open, speaks honestly, and does not have personal or hidden motives. The real you can be known because you are not trying to trick or fool anyone. This person is easy to understand, available and visible. What you see is what you get; nothing hidden lurks in the shadows.

A:5 Consistency

This is about being and doing the same way all the time. People can count on you to speak and act in the same manner from moment to moment, situation to situation, person to person. Holding onto the same principles, actions and behaviors no matter what the situation, or who the person. Sometimes this is called being "seamless." You speak and act in the same way all the time.

A6: Confidence

Being sure of something or someone – self, others, situations, actions or ideas including personal values and abilities. It means a person is not uncertain. This isn't about being conceited, prideful or arrogant. Self-confidence is having confidence in self about an ability. Overconfidence is having *undeserved* confidence—believing something or someone is capable when they are not, including self.

A7: Leveragability

"Leveragability" means making the most of things. Everyone has weaknesses, and everyone has strengths. This is about the best use of people's strengths, but also knowing weaknesses (in self and others) and how to prevent those from becoming problems. This isn't about "using people" but about knowing and using their strengths in the best way.

CONNECTIVITY: Doing It Together

Connectivity is about connecting with others to find ways to reach your shared goals and desires for the relationship. It is also about creating and bringing value to people and the relationship in general. It requires reaching out to others with openness, and knowing how people work best together.

Some people seem gifted with a special ability to connect with others. However, this is also an art which can be practiced. There are definite ways in which we can learn to connect with others not only to reach our desired goals, but also for the pure sake of connecting, of being a part of the human story and plugging into the power of relationships.

The PIECES of Connectivity...

C1: Awareness

This is not just about knowing or realizing things. It is not just being aware, it is being *watchful*, knowing your surroundings, knowing the people with whom you are in relationship, and watching *(being alert)* for opportunities for connection. You are sensitive, awake and aware of all you do and say *(self-awareness)*, and all that others do and say *(others-awareness)*, so connections can be strong.

C2: Affirmation

Positive statements (or actions) and positive attitudes about things, and people. These are used to show approval, and confirm someone's value. It is not just "lip service" (only saying nice things to get something in return). The person who practices affirmation truly believes in the value or truth of something or someone, and is willing to state or share it openly, and appropriately.

C3: Empathy

The ability to recognize, understand and be sensitive to feelings, thoughts and experiences of others. Empathy goes beyond mere sympathy, pity or knowledge of another's emotions or values. It is the ability to "put yourself into another's shoes," to truly feel their emotions and relate to where they are. It is being able to understand how it feels to be someone else. Empathy is very important for making good connections.

C4: Interactional Know-How

Interaction is two or more things, or people, acting together, and having an effect on one another. Know-how is knowledge, so Interactional Know-How is about knowing how interactions work best. It's knowing how people can work together in the best ways, including how they influence each other, and how they impact each other in any relationship.

C5: Collaboration

Collaboration is about "co-laboring" together. It is having an attitude and willingness to work well together for the best results in the relationship. This is true even when there are disagreements. Collaboration looks for common ground to reach goals, and finds ways to partner together for the best possible results. Collaboration is also understanding that when people work well together, the results will be bigger and better than if they worked alone.

C6: Innovation

Innovation is about finding new and better ways to do something. Here in the Connectivity part, it means looking for better ways to connect to get results. Innovation is also being open to new ideas, being creative, and using fresh thinking to connect with others in new and different ways.

C7: Regeneration

Real Connectivity depends on solid individual connections. But sometimes in relationships "disconnects" will happen. If these broken connections are not given attention, Connectivity is weakened, and can even lead to more disconnects. Even one broken link (or "disconnect") can be disastrous. Regeneration is aware of the strength and health of all connections, and comes up with a plan to fix them. This isn't about just slapping a patch on something. It requires the connection to be created again from scratch to provide a connection even stronger than before.

EMPOWERMENT: Boosting Success

Empowerment helps others be stronger and accomplish more. It looks for ways to challenge people to grow, and supports them in these goals. It motivates others to take "good" risks, to see and do new things, and experience more responsibility. People in relationship need to set boundaries for empowerment, for learning, and for new responsibilities. Trust plays a big role, and begins with shared understanding of what is expected, commitments to goals, roles, and even possible consequences when things don't go as expected.

The PIECES of Empowerment...

E1: Initiative

This is about taking the first step or action, which leads to more action. It means you have a willingness to act first. It is a personal decision, not a command. It's taking the opening steps toward making something better. Initiative is the first action toward something, but it doesn't end there. Often taking the first step toward something helps others follow and do their parts also.

E2: Systems Know How

Anywhere a relationship exists, there are "puzzle pieces" that fit together to make things work. Systems Know How means you know about, and understand all these pieces, how they are supposed to work together to benefit the relationship, and then using that knowledge to help keep things on track. This means you take all these different pieces and consider them in your planning, before your doing. It is knowledge of the "entire system" that makes up a relationship and making sure everything works right. *How does everything in the relationship work together? How do these things work best together? What actions have what effect on other actions or people?*

E3: Resource Management
Again, whether in business or personal relationships, there are "resources" available for the day-to-day "work" of the relationship in order to gain the results you want. These can be material things, or it can be people and their skills and abilities. Management means that you make the best use of these resources. You make the best use of people, their abilities, knowledge, experiences, advice and guidance. You have to know people well to manage all your resources well.

E4: Development
This is helping others to grow stronger, get new skills, and improve in general. Careful thought is given to what each person needs, not a "one size fits all" sort of development. Development requires taking the time to really know people, and what will help their growth—then making those opportunities available to them.

E5: Experimentation

This means looking for better ways to do things, and testing to see if a new way works better. Sometimes problems require us to try new ways to solve them. Discovering better ways to do things may take a lot of "trial and error" before finding the best ways. Experimentation should be with a positive attitude that something better will come from the testing of new things. Time and courage are needed for this as well. It also requires allowing time and opportunity for others to make their discoveries.

E6: Reframing

When we view the world around us, we are "framing" it based on our ideas and values. It is our personal way of understanding things. But sometimes our ways of understanding or framing things are not the same as others. RE-framing is remaining open to other viewpoints and outlooks. We need to practice to keep our own ideas from closing doors of understanding. We set aside our ideas to be open to those of others. It is looking at people and things in a new and different way.

E7: Recognition

This is being able to see good work, or something good in others, and then appreciating it in a public way. We let others know we are aware of the good things they have done or are doing, and that their work is appreciated. This always encourages more good work, motivation, responsibility or whatever the good thing is that was observed (attitudes, etc.).

All the parts and pieces of the G.R.A.C.E. at Work Model are presented in a simple chart on the next pages.

The PARTS and PIECES of G.R.A.C.E. at Work

G: GOODWILL makes all the other parts of G.R.A.C.E. work. You make everything all right, no matter what happens in the relationship.

G1: POSITIVISM	Being positive, with positive intent
G2: NON-JUDGMENT	Not judging
G3: SUPPORT	Looking out for each other
G4: GIVING FREELY	Giving without strings
G5: FORGIVENESS	Forgiving without hard feelings
G6: PEACE	Being at peace, keeping peace
G7: GRATITUDE	Being thankful

R: RESULTS has "3R's:" Reason, Relationship and Results. The *reason* for being in a *relationship*, where certain *results* are known and desired.

R1: SHARED PURPOSE	Having shared purpose
R2: DESIRED OUTCOMES	Knowing what you want to get
R3: WHY/WHO BALANCE	Balanced focus on people/product
R4: KNOWN ASSUMPTIONS	Knowing what others believe
R5: EQUAL CONTRIBUTION	Everyone doing their part
R6: ACTION PLANS	Making action plans for results
R7: PERFORMANCE	Working the plan, measuring results

AUTHENTICITY is being real. Knowing yourself first, then how to share "you" with others. Doing what is important to you, and others.

A1: SINCERITY	Being sincere and honest
A2: HUMILITY	Being humble, not arrogant
A3: RESPONSIBILITY/ ACCOUNTABILITY	Doing what's expected (responsible), being "answerable"
A4: TRANSPARENCY	Being an "open book"
A5: CONSISTENCY	Being, acting the same at all times
A6: CONFIDENCE	Being certain of self/others
A7: LEVERAGABILITY	Using strengths, correcting for weaknesses

C: CONNECTIVITY is finding ways to relate to and understand others. Knowing things important to others, wanting to connect with them.	
C1: AWARENESS	Being aware of self and others
C2: AFFIRMATION	Building up others
C3: EMPATHY	Knowing and understanding others
C4: INTERACTIONAL KNOW-HOW	Knowing how people work best together
C5: COLLABORATION	Working together to get results
C6: INNOVATION	Finding better ways to connect
C7: REGENERATION	Fixing broken connections

E: EMPOWERMENT is helping others, and self, to be successful. Overcoming difficulties, seeing possibilities, learning along the way and keeping the "big picture" in sight always.	
E1: INITIATIVE	Ready to act to make things better
E2: SYSTEMS KNOW-HOW	Keeping all the parts working well
E3: RESOURCE MANAGEMENT	Using your resources well
E4: DEVELOPMENT	Helping others grow
E5: EXPERIMENTATION	Experimenting to get better results
E6: REFRAMING	Re-thinking with an open mind
E7: RECOGNITION	Knowing good work, awarding it

If any one of these parts or pieces is missing, there is no G.R.A.C.E.

"Authenticity is a collection of choices that we have to make every day. It's about the choice to show up and be real. The choice to be honest. The choice to let our true selves be seen."

Brené Brown

AUTHENTICITY: Let's Get Real

Being real – *and being all that you can be* – is important in any relationship, but especially in one where you expect real results.

Positive attitudes, and a desire to be exactly who we are, are at the heart of good relationships, and necessary for open and productive communication. Authenticity is the true reality of a person. It is "knowing and showing" the real you. As a part of the G.R.A.C.E. at Work model, it gives life to all the others. If we are not ourselves, then all our efforts of G.R.A.C.E. will not be real, and certainly not successful. *G.R.A.C.E. can't be faked*. It relies on our ability to be authentic *(real)*, and act authentically *(real)*.

Authenticity keeps the relationship balanced and healthy. Authenticity is being honest with yourself and others, choosing how you wish to relate to others, saying what your stand is, holding yourself accountable for your actions, being open and stating needs, desires, moods, attitudes, values and feelings–even about the other person. Each person must first know, then "own up" to his or her own reality. Successful relationships are strong when everyone shows exactly who they are, say exactly what they mean, and use the same standards for self and others, and do so in the spirit of Goodwill.

Authenticity and Your Stand

We all have a set of values and beliefs that we use as a basis for our identity and to make decisions. Whether we know it or not, we act in ways that show our values and beliefs. Being authentic means knowing the purpose of your life or work, and what you are willing to take a stand for.

Being, Saying and Doing

Authenticity is also about saying what you're going to do, then doing what you said you were going to do. And if asked, you can explain why you did what you did. So when people look at you, they're looking to see how closely you "walk your talk."

What You See is What You Get

We hear this phrase used often to describe a person's authenticity. Authenticity is not just about walking the talk, it's about talking the truth and walking the truth – about yourself. Authenticity requires us to first know ourselves well – to know what drives us, moves us, hurts us, annoys or angers us, and pleases us. What are our personal values and guidelines? What are our boundaries? Our hopes and goals? Once we understand these things, we are more able to make the choice, and take the risk, to reveal them to others – and be real in communication.

Authentic Presence

The pieces of authenticity blend together in a way that tells the world who we are. We sometimes call this "presence." The typical definition of this word means the state of "being present." But exactly what or who is present? An empty shell, a phony, a personality "constructed" for public viewing, or the authentic *(real)* person? Our authenticity is seen by others as our presence in the world. It is how we show up in the world.

Presence is seen in how we show the pieces of the authenticity part of G.R.A.C.E. at Work. We can only show these things *(Sincerity, Humility, Responsibility and Accountability, Confidence, Consistency, Transparency and Leveragability)* in a real (authentic) way when we have blended our real parts of body, mind, heart and soul. Knowing inner truths about ourselves in these four areas make up what we can call "SELF knowledge."

"To Thine Ownself Be True"

Shakespeare said that. It simply means *be real*, and be true to who you are. Authenticity begins with self knowledge, and the desire to be true to self. Authenticity, and authentic presence, require the successful blending of body, mind, heart and soul. This is the only thing that makes authenticity possible. This "true you" is then seen as a powerful presence. If the desire to be true to self is missing, a person will never blend and show those core parts (body, mind, heart, and soul), and will most likely have trouble practicing or exhibiting the seven pieces of Authenticity. This person will always struggle with communication.

Presence is the visible way in which we choose to give life to our body, mind, heart and soul. Presence is something we do on purpose – it doesn't just happen. Will we show the "real" us, or a phony? If we plan to be in relationship with others, or plan to communicate in any way, in any place, we will "present a presence" whether we realize it or not. If we are not seen as real and authentic, we will not get the results we want. Many people think presence is only the visible and outward ability to speak well and look good. Those things can help, but real presence comes from being real in body, mind, heart and soul. Authentic presence tells others:

- **Who we are**
- **What we stand for**
- **Where we are going**
- **What we are willing to do to be true to self**

Authentic presence can speak to someone else's body, mind, heart and soul, and make connections. In fact, real presence is the ability to make those body, mind, heart and soul connections in order to communicate with others, and be in relationship. It is true that some people seem to have a natural presence. They just seem to connect well with others. It is likely, though, that this ability didn't start out this way, but only happened when they blended the real parts of their bodies, minds, hearts and souls.

Blending Body, Mind, Heart and Soul

Body, mind, heart and soul combine to make our whole selves. When they all blend and work together, we are living authentically – being "real." Of these "parts of us" the *soul is what shows our presence.* The body, mind, heart and soul are what *connect us to others*.

The **heart** is the emotional side of who we are. It tells us how we feel about the world, and about life in general. It shows our mood, our feelings, and our emotions. Some people try to hide this area, but that means they are only going through the mechanical motions of life. Life is easier, and relationships more successful, when we understand our emotions and how to control them and share them in right ways. It is important to also understand the emotions and feelings of others, allowing others to express them honestly and appropriately.

The **mind** is that big collection of all the facts and things we know, or have experienced. It is often called the "intellect." It is all the bits and pieces of information, how we have interpreted them, and how they are shaped into our ideas and perceptions. It is all the knowledge we have collected over the years and is used to determine our thinking processes. The mind shows what we pay attention to, and will often take control of our relationships. Depending on the way we think, we can either open doors of opportunity, or close them. The mind is usually the chief decision making part of us and sometimes it only provides us incomplete and incorrect information about those decisions.

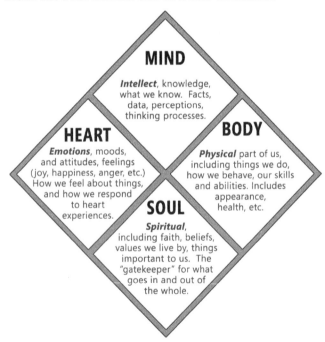

MIND
Intellect, knowledge, what we know. Facts, data, perceptions, thinking processes.

HEART
Emotions, moods, and attitudes, feelings (joy, happiness, anger, etc.) How we feel about things, and how we respond to heart experiences.

BODY
Physical part of us, including things we do, how we behave, our skills and abilities. Includes appearance, health, etc.

SOUL
Spiritual, including faith, beliefs, values we live by, things important to us. The "gatekeeper" for what goes in and out of the whole.

The **soul** contains all the things we believe in, and is the spiritual side of us. It includes our faith (and how that plays a role, or not, in how we think, act, or speak). It includes our values and core beliefs – all the things that are most important to us. These are the things that shape who we are, and are the driving force behind how we show up in the world. The soul reveals our purpose and passion in life. To be truly at peace, and know happiness, comes from the soul's desires. In a way, the soul is like the "gatekeeper" or a guard at the gate of our most inner places. It determines what comes in, and what goes out. It preserves what is most important to us.

The **body** is physical side of who we are. It shows how we behave, how we act. It's the part of us that is seen and heard by others, and by which most people will form their ideas about us. The body is the "spokes-piece" for the mind, heart and soul. It is the place where we will see "side-effects" for not being real and not blending and balancing body, mind, heart and soul into one real, authentic self. This is seen in health issues, stress, and generally not being physically well. If we ignore one part of us, the other parts will scream for attention.

It is important to remember that the "blending" of these parts of us also requires *balancing* them. Often we will allow one part to have too much weight in our thinking or decision making. For example, the mind can override the heart or the soul, and that can cause all parts to suffer, and will have an effect on our relationships as well.

OUR PERSONAL PARTS				OUR AUTHENTICITY **What Others See**
BODY	**MIND**	**HEART**	**SOUL**	
Absent	x	x	x	Not walking the talk (being/doing don't match), mixed messages
x	**Absent**	x	x	Spontaneous ("off the cuff"), not rational
x	x	**Absent**	x	Merely going through the motions, no emotional evidence
x	x	x	**Absent**	Material (physical) life only, no passion or purpose
x	x	x	x	**The ultimate REAL Presence, fully blended and balanced parts**

So how do we get to that place of having a blended, and balanced, body, mind, heart and soul? It begins with SELF Knowledge, and self-diagnosis to learn the truth about who we are, and who we want to be. Those two things may not be the same.

A good place to start is to look at these questions on the next pages for each part of you. Do you already know the answers, or do you need to do some work to discover them, to know the honest truth about yourself, and then to *shape them into what you want to be?*

AREA (Part of Me)	Helps me Know and Understand:	Internal Questions for Personal and Professional Authenticity
BODY (Physical)	How I **ACT** (or behave) in life (or certain times/certain people)	• How does my body allow me to influence the world? • What kind of presence am I creating in the places where I work or live? • How comfortable am I in the presence of others? • What new skills and competencies would give me greater confidence and influence in the world? • How well am I taking care of nutritional needs? • How well am I taking care of my sleep needs? • How well am I doing with physical fitness? • What do I notice about stress in my body, and what do I do about it?
MIND (Intellect)	How I **THINK** about life (or specific issues, people, etc.)	• What information do I pay attention to and what are the consequences of my thinking? • What do I notice about my language i.e., am I using encouraging language that creates possibilities or am I using language that is self-defeating? • How am I keeping myself current with information in the world that I am living in? • How well can I present a logical and convincing argument for what I want to accomplish? • What do I notice about my ability to consider several different perspectives about things?

AREA (Part of Me)	Helps me Know and Understand:	Internal Questions for Personal and Professional Authenticity
HEART (Emotions)	How I **FEEL** about life (or specific issues, people, etc.)	• How well do I understand my emotions and how well do I make them work for me? • How well am I able to know what I am feeling? • How well am I able to show my emotions? • What do I know about what triggers my emotions? • How well am I able to resolve/deal with my emotions? • What do I notice about how my emotions impact others around me? • How well do I recover when I get knocked off balance? • What levels out my emotions after I've been knocked off balance?
SOUL (Spiritual)	The MEANING of life to me, (what is of value and importance to me)	• Who do I declare myself to be? • What is most important in my life? • What is my purpose/passion in life? • What are the principles/values that guide my life? • How do I resolve things in opposition to my principles and values? • What do I believe about transformation in life? i.e. what brings about growth and change in my life and the lives of others? • What am I tolerating (putting up with) and why?

Discovering Values

We all have a set of values, principles and beliefs that make up the foundation of who we are – our authenticity or reality. These values live in the soul, and help us make decisions, share honestly, shape our passion and purpose and drives the other parts of ourselves – the body, mind and heart. Whether we know it or not, we usually act and think in ways that match our values and beliefs. Yet sometimes people have a hard time identifying those values. Can you identify yours? Do you know why you make certain decisions or why you act the way you do? It is always helpful to take some time to discover our values so we can be true to ourselves, and show others our true self – be authentic. This is SELF Knowledge.

Next is a long list of some of the most common values, principles and core beliefs. Check the ones that you believe are part of your soul, part of who you are – the ones most important to you. You might think this is a simple exercise, not necessary or a waste of time. But knowing your values and what makes up who you really are is always important, and the first step in SELF knowledge.

Instructions:

1. Look over this list of 100 values. Think about each one and put a check mark in the boxes that you think are your values and beliefs. There is space to add up to 10 more that may not be included in this list.

2. Look at the values you checked. Now try to narrow them down to your TOP 10 values. Write them in the table below the list.

3. *Now it gets harder.* Look at your list of TOP 10 values. Now rank them in order of importance to you, and list only the TOP 5 in the next table.

1		Accomplishment	27		Direction, Purpose
2		Accountability	28		Discipline
3		Accuracy	29		Diversity
4		Acknowledgement/ Reward	30		Efficiency
			31		Empowerment of others
5		Authenticity	32		Environment
6		Balanced life	33		Equality
7		Best Performance	34		Ethics
8		Challenge	35		Excellence
9		Change	36		Fairness
10		Collaboration (Teamwork)	37		Faith
11		Commitment	38		Family
12		Communication	39		Flair
13		Community	40		Flexibility
14		Compassion	41		Freedom
15		Competence	42		Friendliness
16		Competition	43		Fun
17		Concern for Others	44		Generosity
18		Consensus	45		Goodwill
19		Continuing Learning and improvement	46		Happiness
			47		Hard Work
20		Control	48		Harmony (Peace)
21		Cooperation	49		Health and Well-Being
22		Courage	50		Honesty, Truthfulness
23		Courtesy	51		Honor
24		Creativity	52		Independence
25		Decisiveness	53		Individuality
26		Developing Others	54		Inner Calm, Peace

55		Innovation	83		Safety
56		Intelligence	84		Security
57		Integrity	85		Service (to others)
58		Justice	86		Simplicity
59		Knowledge	87		Sincerity
60		Leadership	88		Skill
61		Learning	89		Solitude
62		Loyalty	90		Speed
63		Lifestyle	91		Stability
64		Meaning	92		Status
65		Openness	93		Strength
66		Orderliness	94		Success, Achievement
67		Organization	95		Timeliness
68		Perfection	96		Tolerance
69		Perseverance	97		Trust
70		Personal Growth	98		Values
71		Pleasure	99		Variety
72		Positive Attitude	100		Wisdom
73		Power	101		
74		Practicality	102		
75		Privacy	103		
76		Progress, Improvement	104		
77		Prosperity	105		
78		Quality (of work, etc.)	106		
79		Resourcefulness	107		
80		Respect for Others	108		
81		Responsibility	109		
82		Results-oriented	110		

My TOP 10 Values   My TOP 5 Values

My TOP 10 Values			My TOP 5 Values		
1			1		
2			2		
3			3		
4			4		
5			5		
6					
7					
8					
9					
10					

Did anything surprise you here? Have your values changed at all since the last you thought about them? What difference can this make in your real self – *your authentic self*? Anything you want to change?

NOTES

A Summary Note About Authenticity

Authenticity may be the most complicated of all the five G.R.A.C.E. parts. It has seven main pieces, but it also requires SELF Knowledge. This is a complete understanding of the four things we are made of: Body, Mind, Heart and Soul.

These things are shown to others in visible ways. What others see of us *(as we behave in ways that show our bodies, minds, hearts, and souls)* can be called "Presence."

Authenticity is being real all the time, but if we don't know ourselves well, it is impossible to be real. The real you is found in your body, mind, heart and soul. Who you are shows up first in the body. It is what people notice first. How you take care of yourself, how you talk, how you act and react are a glimpse into the real you. It is next seen in your mind, the way you think, your ideas and what you pay attention to. Beyond the mind is the heart, which is seen in your moods and emotions. It shows others how you feel about the world, or them. And at the base of it all, is your soul. Here is where what is truly valuable to you is seen in your faith declarations, values, and life's purpose and passion. Whatever the soul is committed to will shape what your body, mind, and heart will pay attention to.

Authenticity + Connectivity = Empowerment

Authenticity and Presence are useless by themselves. We have to make connections with others for them to matter. Our presence is how we show up in the world, and the world is made up of other people. So, by its very nature, connectivity is required to use authenticity and presence.

Knowing and showing *ourselves* authentically is only one part of accomplishing our passion and purpose, and reaching the goals and desired outcomes of any relationship. The other part is knowing *(and many times showing)* others as well.

On the G.R.A.C.E. at Work model, the heart of Authenticity is SELF knowledge *(knowing who you really are)*. The heart of Connectivity is OTHER Knowledge *(knowing who others really are)*. Both kinds of knowledge are needed to have any good relationship. There is a line that runs between the Authenticity and the Connectivity parts. This line is called *trust*.

AUTHENTICITY requires knowing what I am feeling, thinking and doing. CONNECTIVITY requires that I also know what the other person is feeling, thinking and doing. Authenticity is linked with Connectivity. Presence is not a one way, dead-end street.

"Self Knowledge" is the heart of Authenticity, and the center of Connectivity is "Other Knowledge."

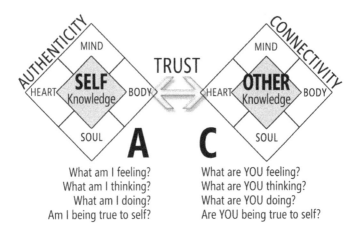

The focus of successful *Empowerment* is combined Self and Other Knowledge, which we can call "Us Knowledge." Before empowerment can happen, all people in the relationship must have a reasonable knowledge of each other – what makes each person "tick" and work best. This "Us Knowledge" helps people work best *together (click!)*, and that empowers them to real desired goals.

It can be summed up with these questions:

Who am I?

Who are you?

What are we together?

And then, *how can we empower each other to have the results we want?*

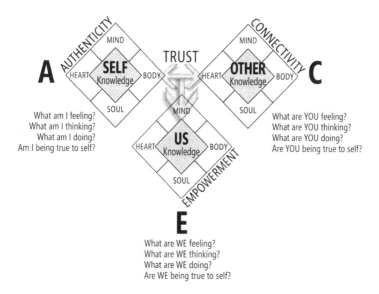

Once both SELF and OTHER Knowledge is joined through trust it produces US Knowledge. This joining can empower both the individuals in relationship, and the relationship itself, to achieve greater results.

And if all this *self, other* and *us* knowledge is combined with ever-present Goodwill, you will most likely achieve the results both parties or people want – and even more – in any relationship.

Without Empowerment *(the product of Authenticity and Connectivity)* people in relationships will only "go through the motions," never getting desired results. And, at some point, even those motions will stop, *and so will the relationship.*

G.R.A.C.E. at Work in Conversations

Conversations are the lifeblood
of relationships. They hold everything together.

No matter what the conversation is about, it can
be more productive, more powerful, and yield
much better results when we practice the 5 parts of
G.R.A.C.E. at Work. Before we focus on the G.R.A.C.E.
at Work foundation for your conversations, let's take
a look at a few tools that can be helpful.

Facts and Opinions

We sometimes confuse facts, opinions and personal
ideas. Facts are things that are true and can be
shown to be true *(not our own interpretation of
those facts.)* Opinions and personal ideas are not
necessarily facts, and may not be shared by others.
Facts and opinions are two different things. It is
sometimes important to make sure we express our
opinions as opinions, not as facts. Understanding
the differences between these two things, and how
we say both of them, can make a huge difference.

Also understand that "our facts" may not be
someone else's facts. For example, one person can
say *"It's hot in here"* and that is their fact, their truth.
The other person may think it's just right, or even
cool. That is *their* fact.

People can agree that the temperature in the room is 72 degrees F *(fact)*, but they may differ greatly on what that means to them *(opinion)*.

Requests and Agreements

It is often necessary in conversation to make a request, or ask for something to be done. It seems like that should be clear enough, but to get the best results, there must be agreement between all parties, and *clear understanding*. Here's a few simple "rules of thumb" to use:

1. Be very specific when describing what you want, or what you want done.

2. Be very specific about who you are requesting to do this.

3. Be sure to state the things that mean you are satisfied with the request you have made (for example, timing, outcomes, methods, etc.)

4. Make sure the other person understands the request, and is in agreement with your stated terms.

These are what we call "clear agreements." Everyone understands the same things, and agrees to them. Sometimes we think we have made a request, but it was not stated as a request. For example, we can say, *"The last time we did this you were very late."* In our minds we think we have requested the other person to be on time, but that request was never made. Only a fact was stated.

Don't assume others understood your statement of fact to be a request. Be clear and straightforward and make a request: *"Please be here on time."*

It is also very important to understand the difference between a *command* and a *request*. A command does not give the other person the right to say *no* or negotiate. A *request* allows the other person the flexibility to say *yes* or *no*, or negotiate the terms. This provides "breathing room" in the relationship.

Expectations and Agreements

We can talk about expectations, and think them, but we must understand that an *expectation is not an agreement*. If you don't have a solid agreement, you don't have any basis for accountability or a clear understanding of the other person's level of commitment or enthusiasm for whatever you're doing. You also don't have any guarantee that the other person will actually do what you expect.

A solid agreement answers questions about the 5W's of responsibility and accountability:

1. **Who,** *has to do*
2. **What,** *by*
3. **When and How**
4. **Well,** *for the sake of (and)*
5. **Why**

Win-Win agreements result from a conversation involving requests. They can become the basis for successful personal or business relationships. A solid agreement should have value and meaning for each person, and that value and meaning should be clear to everyone.

We can think of a relationship as a bank account of sorts, from which we can make withdrawals and deposits. A solid agreement that results in each person getting what they want and expect, means making deposits of Goodwill and trust in your "account." An agreement that ends up with results less than what each wanted means you have taken a withdrawal of trust and Goodwill. The relationship then becomes "smaller," less productive and less satisfying because trust and Goodwill are less.

When we deliver on our agreements, and we're really looking out for the best interests of others, we are telling them we are committed to our relationships with them and we can be trusted.

The power and joy of a great conversation isn't just in the give and take of being heard, but in giving and receiving of what every human needs most... deeper human connection.

Using the G.R.A.C.E. at Work Model in Conversation

GOODWILL

The groundwork for any successful conversation is done at the very beginning, and it starts with Goodwill. Without the presence of Goodwill, every conversation is doomed to failure. Goodwill comes even before the conversation begins. You may even want to explore this with the person you are having the conversation with by establishing mutual Goodwill (everyone in the conversation).

1. How much Goodwill am I willing to give?

2. How much Goodwill are YOU willing to give?

3. What does Goodwill mean to YOU, ME, and US?

The presence of Goodwill in everyone provides the "safe place" for trust in the conversation. If there are issues that come up right at the beginning about Goodwill or the lack of it, deal with them immediately, openly, and WITH Goodwill!

RESULTS

Some conversations don't always have immediately identifiable desired results. Some have very specific expected outcomes. Those that are spontaneous, without stated outcomes, should also be based in the G.R.A.C.E. at Work model, since often conversations go from one thing to another thing, and results can change. Our desired outcomes should always be for the good of the relationship, even in those spontaneous talks. But for those conversations where there is obviously a desired result, that result should be discussed up front. Explore these questions before discussion:

1. What do I (WE) want to accomplish in this conversation?

2. What is the big picture here?

3. What are our desired results?

4. Why are we having this conversation?

Let everyone in the conversation discuss these and have their "say." Make sure everyone agrees with the answers. This keeps your conversation on track without veering off into distracting areas that keep you from achieving your desired outcomes.

AUTHENTICITY AND CONNECTIVITY

We've already talked about the important pairing of these two parts of G.R.A.C.E. Go back and review that section about SELF Knowledge, OTHER Knowledge and US Knowledge. Be sure to explore these questions for each person in the conversation:

1. What am I feeling? *(What are YOU feeling?)*

2. What am I thinking? *(What are YOU thinking?)*

3. What do I want? *(What do YOU want?)*

4. What am I doing? *(What are YOU doing?)*

Usually the biggest part of the conversation happens here – as these questions are explored with honesty and openness – because you have created a safe place for people to share. You have already established Goodwill where this can happen.

EMPOWERMENT

Here is where the ME and YOU becomes WE or US. You have already talked about your desired outcomes. And now you know how everyone feels, what they are thinking, and what they will do. It's time here to make a plan for how to measure and get to your expected results.

1. What are WE feeling?

2. What are WE thinking?

3. What do WE want?

4. What are WE doing?

(Are we all on the same page?)

5 Simple Steps to Powerful Conversations

1. GOODWILL
Agree to work through the conversation with Goodwill. If necessary remind everyone of this, and take a look at what pieces of Goodwill are needed.

2. RESULTS
What is the "big picture" bringing you together in conversation? What are the desired results *(describe them fully)*. Get agreement.

3. AUTHENTICITY
What does this big picture mean to each person? What are the moods, feelings and attitudes about all of this *(for each person involved)*? Honor and respect one another to create a place of trust and sharing.

4. CONNECTIVITY
Make connections with each other. Connect all the pieces of information needed to reach expected results. How are the people connected? What are the challenges? "Connect all the dots" on this conversation.

5. EMPOWERMENT
Take all you have discussed together and make a plan that everyone agrees to. Work the plan, together, and measure progress. Empower one another to success.

CONVERSATION "TIPS"

1. *Remember that each of us is made up of body, mind, heart and soul.* We always operate from their combined input. Understand that this is also true for others. When we are in conversation, there will be many hearts, minds, souls and bodies interacting. All of them are worth considering.

2. *Share yourself on all levels, but in a way that doesn't judge others.* Let others share themselves on all levels also. Try not to over-analyze or judge anything. Question, but don't judge, the things you don't understand.

3. *Actively try to find those places where you can connect with others as you share.*

4. *Give good feedback.* Feedback is sharing what you have heard or seen, from your perspective. Good feedback is constructive, meaning it will help the other person. Bad feedback is nothing more than judgment. Feedback should be about the issues you are discussing, based on your observations.

   • Be direct, and don't beat around the bush.

   • Remember feedback is often only your *opinion*, not a fact. Don't hold it too tightly.

- Try not to make feedback positive or negative. Think of it, and speak of it, as observation only, not judgment.

- Always begin your feedback with "I" and not "you." Say *"I have seen or observed…"* not *"you have,"* or *"you need…"*

- Be pleasant and offer your feedback in Goodwill, but don't fake it. People will see right through that.

- Let your words and your body language be pleasant and non-threatening.

5. *Ask the right questions, at the right time, and in the right way.*

- Don't ask unnecessary questions. Focus on what is important to both of you, and always start from a place of Goodwill.

- Don't interrogate *(like a police detective!)*.

- Keep your own agenda out of your questions.

- Ask questions when something isn't clear, or you need to know more about what the other person is thinking.

- Ask "what and how" questions. Try to avoid the "why" questions because those are often difficult to answer and involve personal feelings. Sometimes the "why" questions need to be asked, but try to limit them, and ask them only in a safe place of G.R.A.C.E. where shared trust can give you the answers you need.

- Ask questions that are designed to help the other person think differently about the situation, or help them explore the issues better. Sometimes questions can help open up another person's thinking about things to explore new thoughts and ideas.

- Don't try to disguise your desire to tell the other person what to do by asking questions like *"don't you think it's a great idea if you tried..."* or others like this that show what YOU think, not what the other person thinks.

- Don't try to solve problems too quickly. Give plenty of time for everything to be said that needs to be said. Make sure you have explored all the important issues before trying to solve any difficult issues.

- Give enough time for silence as a response from the other person. Sometimes he or she will need to think first before responding. Don't pressure them to answer immediately.

- Watch for emotional responses. It's possible you have touched something deeper and of great importance. Use care and respect when questioning further.

6. *Listen well, and hear it all.* Talking is not the only part of conversation. Talk goes two ways, and for one to talk, the other must listen. Listening and hearing are two different things. We can act sometimes like we are listening, and we may even hear the words being spoken, but hearing means we understand and know what the other person is really saying. When others are speaking, either to answer our questions or to just say what they need to say, we should show respect for what they say by getting rid of the distractions that keep us from fully hearing them

"The art of conversation is the art of hearing as well as of being heard."
William Hazlitt

(including our own thoughts), and giving our entire attention to not only listening, but really hearing what they mean to say.

• Some people think they are listening by not speaking, but inside all they are doing is planning their own responses and what they will say next. This is annoying, disrespectful and keeps us from really hearing. Most people can tell when we do this and they don't like it. This is a distraction we can control by giving our ears (and our minds and hearts) fully to the other person's words.

• When you listen, look for new ways you can connect with the other person to know them better.

- Do a mental self-check. Are you really ready to listen and hear the other person, or do you need an attitude check?

- Remember the conversation isn't likely about you. You are listening and hearing to help another person.

- Don't hurry the other person by interrupting, and don't take up too much of the "air time" with your own talk. If you happen to be talking more than the other person *(or anyone else)*, you aren't really listening and hearing. Ask yourself this question, remembered by the initials W.A.I.T: *"Why Am I Talking?"* [1]

- Listen for what really matters to the other person, and not what you think you want to hear or say.

- Also listen for what was said, but also what was not said. Sometimes we expect certain responses to things but the information offered is not complete for some reason. When someone avoids questions by round about conversation, that indicates something needs further exploration, but with caution, especially regarding personal feelings. As indicated above, this is a place to proceed with caution and respect.

- And always listen to hear new things about the person you are speaking with, things that help you better understand and connect with them.

The Difficult Conversation

We've all had them, and we will most likely have them again. Using G.R.A.C.E. at Work for a difficult conversation is the same as using it for any conversation. Think of your difficult conversation as any conversation, but one that has a few more things to be talked about and worked through. Use the steps outlined above, but also think (and talk) through these issues as well:

1. When and how did Goodwill break down? Describe it, and how it affected the relationship.

2. Again, agree to work together with Goodwill. Use it EVERY step in this conversation. Right from the start talk about what pieces of Goodwill are needed here.

3. How much Goodwill do you have to work with now? How can it be increased?

4. Say what is important to you, and give others that chance too. Determine what is important for everyone.

5. Was there a breakdown in intent *(what was in mind originally)*, and impact *(how it affected someone else)*? Work through any issues here.

6. What can you agree on?

7. Be real, and be "visible" or what is called transparent. No hidden agendas. Agree to an open discussion, without argument or blame.

8. Be careful with your words, and your body language. Sometimes we speak louder with our bodies than with our mouths. Be sure to work through the Authenticity-Connectivity-Empowerment instructions provided earlier.

9. Sort out who "owns" what, what responsibilities or accountabilities are needed *(no blaming!)*. But do this only after Goodwill is firmly in place.

10. Make a plan for reconciliation, any change in action plans, and again your desired results. What things need to change, and how? How can you reach your goals now? Come to an agreement to move forward from here.

Remember that the conversation is not complete until you move through the Empowerment part. This is where all the talk up to this point has prepared you to actually move forward, to get past the "difficult" place. Without the Empowerment part, it's just all talk. This is where opportunities are explored and plans are made together.

Whatever the reason, difficult conversations can be managed to become powerful conversations instead – often with very surprising, and pleasing, results. But as always, this is possible only if Goodwill is present right from the start. While Authenticity and Connectivity go together to produce Empowerment to get Results, none of it works if Goodwill is not present right from the start.

Perhaps one of the most important "tips" for difficult conversations is this: DON'T GIVE UP! Successful relationships are always changing and growing. They never stand still. They require a lot of work and energy – and more conversations.

Relationships need forward momentum or they will roll downhill and stop. When we increase the things that build forward momentum *(empowerment)* we will decrease the things that keep us from moving forward. Sometimes one difficult conversation doesn't get you where you want to be. Keep at it. Have another, and another. As long as you continue to practice G.R.A.C.E. at Work, you will find you have fewer and fewer difficult conversations and more rewarding and transforming conversations.

The Internal Conversation

The most overlooked, but also the most practiced, conversations are those we have with ourselves. We call these Internal Conversations. We have these conversations many times a day, every day of our lives. Internal conversations are often triggered by the need to make decisions, to plan the future, or just resolve a certain set of ideas or thinking. These can be very simple, solving problems or making decisions quickly and easily, or they can be very hard, time consuming and exhausting.

As with all relationships, being who we really are (being authentic) is absolutely critical. That means the "inside you" must agree with the "outside you." What you show others needs to be the real inside you. For internal conversations, there is a little different kind of authenticity. We each have two basic sides to us that need to work together in agreement and balance.

There is one side we can call the "internal champion." This champion inside us is the part of us that feels good, strong, confident and capable. The other part of us takes the opposite stand – our "internal critic." The critic in us is that part that always brings us down, criticizes our thoughts and actions, and essentially tears down everything the champion builds up. There is a struggle between these two parts of us in every internal conversation.

Quite often we allow one or the other of these sides of us to be the loudest voice. Sometimes the internal critic will drown out the internal champion. And sometimes it is the other way around. The battle between these two internal selves is the hardest part of an internal conversation. Learning how to recognize and balance these two sides that live in each of us is the key.

IDENTIFYING YOUR INTERNAL CRITIC
AND INTERNAL CHAMPION

Your Internal Critic	Your Internal Champion
Thinks it's all or nothing	Finds "middle ground"
Sees things purely in black and white	Thinks more in "shades of gray"
Thinks one bad thing is a pattern of defeat	Tests thoughts to see how true they are (asks others)
Rejects good things because "they don't count"	Identifies partial success (not complete failure)
Jumps to negative conclusions/few or no facts	Trusts the facts
Exaggerates inappropriately	Thinks/speaks less emotionally charged
Attaches negative labels to people, behavior, events	Thinks through feelings (emotions/inner thoughts) before outwardly responding
Sees self as the cause of negative things	Gives self same advice as would give a friend
No self Goodwill	Willing to "give self a break" – extend goodwill

Listening only to your Internal Critic results in self condemnation and no forward movement. You're stuck and buried under a pile of blame and guilt. Listening only to your Internal Champion can result in "pie in the sky" or unrealistic expectations of self and possibly ultimate failures. The only way to successfully move forward is a balanced, realistic evaluation of what both voices are saying to find the "real you" – a blend of both the critic and the champion.

Goodwill is where every successful conversation must begin and end and it is the same for internal conversations. Unfortunately it always seems easier to extend Goodwill to others than to self. When we finally decide to accept personal Goodwill, we are empowered to change the unrealistically tough Internal Critic into a constructive and honest critic that can work with and balance our Internal Champion to achieve real results.

The same ideas that help guide a successful conversation with others also help us have more productive – and far less painful – internal conversations. Try using this checklist to bring your authentic self to internal conversations.

*Taking the time to honestly work through this list can
eliminate the inner turmoil of arriving at desired outcomes.*

Internal Conversation Checklist	
GOODWILL	
1	How much Goodwill am I willing to give myself?
2	What is the absence of Goodwill doing to my thinking?
3	In what instances, if any, do I find it hard to give myself Goodwill?
4	What does Goodwill look like in my internal conversations?
5	How can I give myself more Goodwill?
RESULTS	
1	What am I trying to accomplish in this internal conversation?
2	What kind of outcomes do I want?
3	Why is this important to me?
4	What is at stake if I don't have this internal conversation?
5	What else in my life is affected by this?
AUTHENTICITY	
1	What am I feeling, thinking?
2	What am I doing, or not doing?
3	How real and honest am I being about my skills, abilities, past experiences, contributions, strengths and weaknesses?
4	What are my potential misconceptions of these things? Have I corrected these, along with hidden agendas and negative thought patterns?
5	What would be the possible unintended consequences of my decisions and choices?

CONNECTIVITY	
1	Am I connected to all parts of me, including my purpose and passion? How can I integrate my being better?
2	Do I really know who I am, and know my true values and beliefs?
3	How can my authentic self help me in this conversation?
4	What information is missing, or what other "gaps" are there in this conversation that I need to connect to?
5	Is there any way others can help me in this internal conversation?
EMPOWERMENT	
1	What is my internal critic saying?
2	What is my internal champion saying?
3	How can I manage and balance the critic and champion in me?
4	Am I jumping to conclusions, making guesses or assuming things (coming to conclusions) with no real evidence?
5	What can I do (or think) to empower myself to move forward?

After working through this list the first time, consider coming up with a simple action plan on how to process these conversations. Maybe just work through the initials G.R.A.C.E and learn to direct grace toward yourself.

Playing in a Bigger Space

The results we get in life depend
on knowing what makes people
work together best.

Results depend on relationships. Good results come from good relationships. G.R.A.C.E. at Work is designed to improve and grow relationships of all kinds. It works because it is based on the principles of human dynamics *(how humans work together)*. Playing in a bigger space is about growing the relationships and enjoying greater results together.

If you want greater (bigger and better) results, you need to play in a bigger space. The first step toward building this space is to take a look at what you have now, and compare it to what you would like to have. The G.R.A.C.E. at Work model lets you test and build plans for growing results. Here's a simple way to begin this growth. Take a look at these questions and give some serious thought to your answers. Start by thinking of just one major relationship in your life. It can be with a fellow worker, a friend, a spouse, or anyone. Focus on one relationship and answer these questions on the next pages. If this exercise works well for you, try answering these questions for *every* relationship in your life.

Testing Your Space *(to Play in a Bigger Space)*

1. How would you describe the space you are currently playing in? (In other words, how would you describe the relationship right now? Does the "space" of it feel right, or are things tight with no room for growth?)

2. What would it mean to you to be playing in a bigger space? Can you describe how this space can be bigger?

3. Who are you connecting with to get your desired results, and for what reason?

4. What results are you currently able to see and realize?

5. What results would you like to be able to realize?

6. Where do you believe you have opportunities to grow your results, or play in a bigger space?

7. Now think about the G.R.A.C.E. at Work parts, and keep in mind your answers to Question 6 above. How do you think showing Goodwill can grow this space, and give better results?

8. How could Authenticity (being real, and who you are) help do this? Who do you need to connect with on a better, more real, level?

9. What opportunities do you have to practice Connectivity with others to improve results?

10. How can you Empower others in this relationship and how will that grow your results?

11. How would you rate yourself on each of the five pieces of the parts of G.R.A.C.E.? How can you grow each of these (how are you displaying them to others)?

12. Where do you feel stress, frustration or lack of potential? How can the G.R.A.C.E. at Work model help with these things?

13. Why can't you get the results you want in your current space? *(i.e., what is missing, or what is getting in the way?)*

14. How can you use your purpose and passion with others to get better results?

15. What parts and pieces of G.R.A.C.E. do you think are currently missing in this relationship?

Building and growing results depends on building and growing relationships. Try sketching out a quick worksheet showing a diamond shape *(see figure page 76),* with the G.R.A.C.E. components listed. Jot down your current results in the "today" box, then write words to show bigger and better results in the bigger diamond. This works for any relationship. How can you get this bigger space, and these bigger results, by using each of the five G.R.A.C.E. parts?

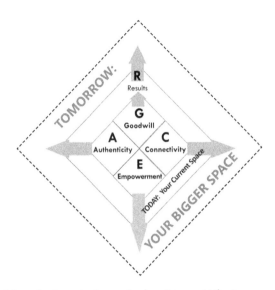

Now let's get down to business. *What can you do right now to grow these relationships to get great results?* Use your worksheet and your notes to make a solid plan for growth.

It is eye-opening and useful to try this exercise together with other people in this relationship. Ask them to do the same thing you did with the worksheet and the questions. Often people in relationships have different ideas about these things, and talking about them can bring breakthroughs and changed behaviors that lead to much bigger spaces. No matter what your playing space is *(international business or one or a few individuals),* its growth depends upon relationships and making the most of human connections.

Stuck? Reframing Is The Answer

Can't get where you want to be,

either with self or with others?
Tried playing in a bigger space but always return to the same small place of frustration?

This is when stepping outside the box we have built with our own thoughts, values and ways of doing things can open up huge possibilities for accomplishing goals and growing relationships. Perhaps it's time to loosen the hold on our comfort zones and realize there are other ways of thinking, and other ways of accomplishing goals. It's how we get "unstuck."

We all have our established ways of thinking. But is our way the only way? If we believe that, chances are we will not realize the things we want to achieve, especially in relationships.

The process of getting unstuck is called reframing. That's a technical word for "thinking outside the box." It's about making your "frame" larger to include new ideas, new ways of thinking, new options and new possibilities. Your ways of thinking, speaking, being and doing are the box you have constructed. It's the comfort zone you live in and frequently it keeps you from seeing what is outside the box. The reframing process helps create new options for a new future, one you didn't have before – one you would like to have.

In relationships, one or both people may reach a "stuck" phase. You may need to get yourself unstuck, or you might need to help others reframe to think differently. One of the greatest tools for getting "unstuck" is adding a measure of grace for yourself and/or others. This will often impact your thinking, perspectives and experiences during this time. The absence of Goodwill *(grace, or Goodwill perhaps undeserved)* leaves no room for any benefit of doubt, second chances or even forgiveness. Adding Goodwill here opens doors to new possibilities and opportunities.

Whether for self or others, reframing perspectives helps all of us be more true to ourselves and open to others emotionally, intellectually, physically, and spiritually. It shapes and preserves our authenticity. Reframing can often provide the means to achieving real relationship goals that may have previously been impossible. There is amazing power in grace.

10 Steps to a Bigger Space through Reframing

1. Identify breakthroughs you'd like to accomplish for yourself (and/or other person). Describe the "bigger picture." Why do you need to reframe?

2. Determine the consequences for NOT reframing. What will happen if you don't do this?

3. Identify your values, thoughts, circumstances, perspectives, judgments or anything that may prevent breakthroughs or reaching desired goals.

4. Rethink how you see these things. Explore possibilities beyond previous thinking. Any preconceptions or misconceptions? Any narrow thinking that needs to broaden?

5. Try to see things as others see them. Walk in their shoes. Breakthroughs happen when we finally understand why others believe and do as they do.

6. Decide what you absolutely must embrace and things you are willing to "let go of." What is negotiable, and what is non-negotiable *(with self and others)*.

7. Identify "outside the box" possibilities for inspiration or different ways of thinking/doing things.

8. Understand how these possibilities can enable desired goals. Think them through.

9. Identify challenges in creating a commitment to moving forward. What could keep me or others from committing to this reframe?

10. Keep the G.R.A.C.E. model as structure and balance for your reframing.

SIGNS OF A SUCCESSFUL REFRAME

displaying and building **G.**oodwill

ever-present eye on bigger **R.**esults

refining and growing **A.**uthenticity

seeking and expanding **C.**onnectivity

providing **E.**mpowerment

FOR SELF AND OTHERS

for BIGGER SPACES TO PLAY

"If a problem can't
be solved within the
frame it was conceived,
the solution lies in
reframing the problem."

— Brian McGreevy

A Fall From G.R.A.C.E.

None of us is perfect. Even when we practice G.R.A.C.E. at Work, we will not do it perfectly, especially at first. It is helpful to understand when we have failed at G.R.A.C.E. so we can be prepared to do it better next time. Here are some of the signs that you might have *"fallen from G.R.A.C.E."* Also, for each person, this list might look a little different. Think of other things that might be on *your personal* list of things that show you need to go back and review G.R.A.C.E. at Work and learn from your mistakes.

I have fallen from G.R.A.C.E....

1. When I don't assume positive intent *(I am negative, and don't feel or show Goodwill).*

2. When I do or say something against my declaration of who I am, my values, or beliefs.

3. When I don't accept ownership/responsibility for my actions.

4. When I do or say something that disconnects me from the other person.

5. When I pass judgment on others in ways that prevent coming back together *(reconciliation).*

6. When I hold back information that could have empowered the other person.

7. What I demand is more than what the person is currently able to give.

8. When I refuse to forgive and forget. When I don't let go of past hurts.

9. When I don't give people the honor and respect that should be given.

10. When I contribute to someone else's fall from G.R.A.C.E.

Do you want to add any other "signs" that you need to go back and review the G.R.A.C.E. at Work ways of being in relationships with others? Add them to your own list of reminders below.

1.

2.

3.

4.

5.

G.R.A.C.E. EXERCISES

There are ways to improve how you use the G.R.A.C.E. at Work model with others.

Look in the next section for the G.R.A.C.E. at Work self test. This is a quick way to see where you might be strong, and where you might be weak in the 5 parts of G.R.A.C.E. at Work. Look at your scores on the test. What areas need improvement? Start at those places with the steps below. Here are some ideas to help you discover and improve the power of G.R.A.C.E. at Work in your relationships.

Goodwill Exercises

1. Remember all the people who have had a positive influence on your life, and think about what they did to help you succeed.

2. Think about how fortunate you are to have had the opportunity to connect with and learn from these people. Develop a grateful attitude.

3. If it's still possible, consider contacting them to thank them for their influence in your life.

4. Identify the things you learned that you can use with others to show Goodwill.

5. Think often about what Goodwill really means *(be positive, give without condition, forgive, etc.)* Spend time thinking about each of the seven pieces of Goodwill.

6. Consider why Goodwill is important in relationships.

7. Think about how you can be in a "Goodwill mode" all the time. Figure out how you can overcome any personal roadblocks to Goodwill.

8. Every day, think about all the good things in your life, be thankful, and look for opportunities to share those good things with others.

9. Think about people with whom you have difficulty feeling or showing Goodwill and think about what prevents this. Resolve these issues that are hurdles to Goodwill with others.

10. Think about the things you are doing today, and actively plan how you can show Goodwill to others throughout the day.

Results Exercises

1. Become a master "results oriented" thinker. Think through the things you do, with your desired goals in mind all the time. Think about current relationships. Can you quickly summarize the REASONS for the project/ relationship? What RESULTS do you want? How do these results define the relationship?

2. Consider how others might think about intended goals and results. Is everyone clear? Is everyone "onboard" and in agreement? If not, what can you do about that?

3. Practice being goal-oriented in what you do. *(Keep your mind on what you want to achieve.)*

4. Learn how to create a vision for what you want to do. Make sure it is based in reality, not fantasy. Think through the process of how you will achieve this vision. This takes a little practice!

5. Always communicate your vision and desired results clearly, describing all its parts.

6. Completely explore the responsibilities and accountabilities that are needed to achieve goals and vision. Who is responsible for what? What accountabilities are in place?

7. Communicate roles and responsibilities, and expected accountabilities. Check to see if everyone understands and is committed. Repeat this step often.

8. Figure out what will show your progress, and what you need to check to be sure you are still on the right track. If necessary, adjust your plans, responsibilities, and your understanding of what others are thinking. *Never assume anything!*

9. Daily consider your agenda, identify your goals and desired results, and hold yourself accountable FIRST. *(Practice even with the "small" stuff.)*

10. When you make your plans *(for anything you want to do)*, think through how each step will help you reach your results.

Authenticity Exercises

1. KNOW YOURSELF! Spend some serious time discovering your authentic (real) self, what makes you that way, and who is the REAL you.

2. Understand what being authentic means.

3. Make a choice to be authentic (real) and transparent (open) always, in every relationship.

4. Identify what is most important to you, and what is non-negotiable *(unwilling to compromise)*.

5. Take and declare an open stand on your issues, without "attitude."

6. Hold yourself accountable for your actions and words that support your authentic self, and take responsibility for those actions and words.

7. KNOW OTHERS! Take time to get to really know the people with whom you have relationships. What makes them tick? What are their values and beliefs?

8. Create a safe space where others can also be open, authentic, transparent, accepting and willing to share without fear of judgment, consequences, or rejection.

9. Daily evaluate your agenda, identify your goals and desired results, and hold yourself accountable FIRST.

10. Get honest feedback from others. Honestly evaluate your authenticity often.

Connectivity Exercises

1. People must interact and connect. Train yourself to look for connections, to actively "think connections" so that wherever you are, whomever you are with, you are aware of possible connections now or in the future.

2. Connectivity means finding ways to relate to others, understanding how they feel, what is important to them, and understanding differences, strengths and weaknesses. Try thinking this way all the time. Every time you are with others, be thinking about how can connect with them.

3. Learn how to empathize *(see things through others' eyes)* and find ways to engage them.

4. Look for things you have in common with others and consider those possible connection points through conversation.

5. Know what is important to others. Discover their vision *(hopes, dreams)*, and what might become shared goals.

6. Think beyond the obvious. Connections can exist in places never before considered.

7. Understand how your words and actions affect others. See if these things have the kind of effect you really want on others. Where are the gaps?

8. Practice clearly communicating expectations, responsibilities and accountabilities.

9. Learn to network effectively and continually build connections. Networking is all about making connections, even "off the wall" connections *(you both might love a certain TV show, etc.)* with others.

10. Remember that connections need attention or they will disappear. Know what that looks like for each of your connections, and give them the appropriate attention.

Empowerment Exercises

1. Potential is everywhere, in everyone. Learn how to spot it, seeing beyond the obstacles or the obvious. Practice this everywhere, with everyone.

2. Know the real meaning of empowerment. It does not mean YOU do it, it means you create the environment for others to have success.

3. Like everything else, empowerment requires balance. Know how to motivate and encourage without pressuring, how to guide without stopping personal expression. There are many

such balances when we empower others. Know them, and observe them. Know when to let them go, and when to come alongside.

4. Create a safe space for others to grow. This means building an environment of trust and openness without judgment.

5. Make this thought important to you: *"It's not about me."* When we empower others, it should not be for our own power. It is about helping *others* to grow and succeed. Even when we are working toward shared purpose, empowerment sets self aside so that others may have the spotlight.

6. If necessary, guide yourself and others to reframe how you think about things. This is a powerful form of empowerment.

7. When working together, learn to always talk about each person's expectations, shared commitments, responsibilities and consequences. Don't leave anything out there not discussed or understood.

8. Learn how to use all the things you have available to help yourself and others succeed.

9. Be realistic. Empowerment is often done one step at a time and needs to be based on what is realistically possible.

10. Allow time for growth, learning and reaching potential.

Test Yourself

Sometimes it is very helpful to find out where you are and how you measure up to the guidelines of G.R.A.C.E. at Work.

You can do this through a simple self test – *as long as you are completely honest!*

The following pages show questions for each of the 7 pieces of the 5 parts of G.R.A.C.E. at Work. For each statement, think about how you behave and speak most of the time with others. Don't rate yourself on how you WANT to be, but how you are right now. For example, the first piece of the Goodwill part is G1: Positivism. The statement for this piece is *"I am always positive in how I think, what I say, and what I do. I start with positive intent."*

Is this true for you? How often? Select one of the ratings: *Always, Mostly, Sometimes, Rarely, or Never.* Be sure to be honest because it does not help you grow when you pretend to be something you are not.

Answer all the questions, total your scores, then look for where you are already strong, and where you need some work. Use the blank pages after the test to make notes about what you want to do from here. Write down a plan!

Part G: Goodwill

#	Piece	Statement	Always	Mostly	Sometimes	Rarely	Never
		Rate each statement *(circle the number)* below based on your actual actions and behavior. Be honest! THESE ARE ACTUAL BEHAVIOR RATINGS. *" I behave in a way that shows..."*					
G1	Positivism	I am always positive in how I think, and what I do. I start with positive intent.	4	3	2	1	0
G2	Non-Judgment	I do not judge people, or situations, based on my own thoughts or personal bias. I do not "judge a book by its cover."	4	3	2	1	0
G3	Support	I support others I am in relationship with, and look out for their best interests.	4	3	2	1	0
G4	Generosity	I am generous, and give freely to others without expecting something in return.	4	3	2	1	0
G5	Forgiveness	I am able to forgive a wrong without hard feelings.	4	3	2	1	0
G6	Peace	I am at peace (okay) with "what is" and in harmony in my relationships.	4	3	2	1	0
G7	Gratitude	I have an attitude of thankfulness, and I am able to express gratitude to, and for, others.	4	3	2	1	0
		Totals for each column					
		GRAND TOTAL for Goodwill					

My notes about these statements and my scores:

Part R: Results

#	Piece	Statement	Always	Mostly	Sometimes	Rarely	Never
		Rate each statement *(circle the number)* below based on your actual actions and behavior. Be honest! THESE ARE ACTUAL BEHAVIOR RATINGS. *"I behave in a way that shows..."*					
R1	Shared Purpose	My purpose for being in a relationship is shared with the other person(s).	4	3	2	1	0
R2	Desired Outcomes	I know what I want to get out of my relationships.	4	3	2	1	0
R3	What/Who Balance	I keep a balance of why we are in the relationship with helping those I am in relationship with.	4	3	2	1	0
R4	Known Assumptions	I know what others think about things, and work to get the facts straight.	4	3	2	1	0
R5	Equal Contribution	I do my part in relationships.	4	3	2	1	0
R6	Acton Plans	I make plans for how to get the results I/we want.	4	3	2	1	0
R7	Performance	I work the plan and measure results along the way, making corrections if needed.	4	3	2	1	0
		Totals for each column					
		GRAND TOTAL for Results					

My notes about these statements and my scores:

Part A: Authenticity							
#	**Piece**	**Statement**	**My Rating**				
Rate each statement *(circle the number)* below based on your actual actions and behavior. Be honest! THESE ARE ACTUAL BEHAVIOR RATINGS. *"I behave in a way that shows..."*			Always	Mostly	Sometimes	Rarely	Never
A1	Sincerity	I am sincere and honest in what I say and what I do.	4	3	2	1	0
A2	Humility	I am humble, not proud or arrogant.	4	3	2	1	0
A3	Responsibility/ Accountability	I do what is expected of me, and I am "answerable" for my actions.	4	3	2	1	0
A4	Transparency	I am an "open book." I do not have hidden motives or agendas. What you see is what you get.	4	3	2	1	0
A5	Consistency	I am the same, in words and actions, at all times.	4	3	2	1	0
A6	Confidence	I am certain of myself, and confident in others I am in relationship with.	4	3	2	1	0
A7	Leveragability	I use my strengths for best results, and correct for weaknesses in myself and others.	4	3	2	1	0
		Totals for each column					
		GRAND TOTAL for Authenticity					

My notes about these statements and my scores:

Part C: Connectivity

#	Piece	Statement	My Rating				
		Rate each statement *(circle the number)* below based on your actual actions and behavior. Be honest! THESE ARE ACTUAL BEHAVIOR RATINGS. *"I behave in a way that shows..."*	Always	Mostly	Sometimes	Rarely	Never
C1	Awareness	I pay attention to things, and I am aware of myself, and others.	4	3	2	1	0
C2	Affirmation	I build up others to help them grow.	4	3	2	1	0
C3	Empathy	I know and understand, and can relate to others.	4	3	2	1	0
C4	Interactional Know-How	I know how people work best together, and use that information in my relationships.	4	3	2	1	0
C5	Collaboration	I work together with others to get the results we want.	4	3	2	1	0
C6	Innovation	I find better ways to connect and do things together.	4	3	2	1	0
C7	Regeneration	I know when a connection is broken, and I work to fix it.	4	3	2	1	0
		Totals for each column					
		GRAND TOTAL for Connectivity					

My notes about these statements and my scores:

Part E: Empowerment

#	Piece	Statement	My Rating				
		Rate each statement *(circle the number)* below based on your actual actions and behavior. Be honest! THESE ARE ACTUAL BEHAVIOR RATINGS. *"I behave in a way that shows..."*	Always	Mostly	Sometimes	Rarely	Never
E1	Initiative	I am ready to take the first steps and act when necessary to make things better.	4	3	2	1	0
E2	Systems Know-How	I understand how all the parts of a relationship work, and I try to keep them working well.	4	3	2	1	0
E3	Resource Management	I know what resources we have in a relationship, and how to use them the best way.	4	3	2	1	0
E4	Development	I help others grow, using every opportunity to develop them and their abilities.	4	3	2	1	0
E5	Experiment-ation	I experiment with things to get better results.	4	3	2	1	0
E6	Reframing	I am able to re-think things and people with an open mind.	4	3	2	1	0
E7	Recognition	I know good work when I see it, and I reward it in right ways.	4	3	2	1	0
		Totals for each column					
		GRAND TOTAL for Empowerment					

My notes about these statements and my scores:

Notes...

Write down some of your thoughts about the results of your self test.

- What are your strong areas?

- What areas need the most attention?

- How will you plan to improve your weak areas?

Notes...

Now try this. Put yourself in the shoes of someone you are in relationship with. Now go back and rate yourself again the same way, how you behave in certain areas. BUT THIS TIME **DO IT FROM THE OTHER PERSON'S POINT OF VIEW**. How do *they* see you, and how would *they* rate you in these areas? This exercise seems silly, but it can be very eye opening and get us to look at ourselves through the eyes of others – and open doors for personal growth.

• How did you do?

• What surprised you here?

• What can you do about it?

Notes...

CPSIA information can be obtained
at www.ICGtesting.com
Printed in the USA
BVHW050459101022
648874BV00001B/7